SEPTIMUS

TO THE RESCUE

Story by Sheila Digby
Illustrated by Derrick Hughes

A CARLTON HOUSE PUBLICATION

British Library Cataloguing-in-Publication Data.

A catalogue record for this book is available from
the British Library.

First published 1996 by Carlton House.
Second enlarged edition 1998

Published by Carlton House Publications,
56 The Esplanade, Fowey, Cornwall PL23 1JA.

Printed by Penwell Limited, Callington, Cornwall.

Septimus Seagull woke up at his home on the cliffs and looked down at the sea.

A strong wind had started to blow, and the waves were getting big.

Just then, his wife Selena opened her eyes and said she was hungry.

'Yes,' said Septimus, 'I am too. I'll go and look for some breakfast.'

Septimus flew off and landed on a beach nearby.

He had just found a tasty piece of fish when he heard someone shouting 'Help!'

Septimus looked out to sea and saw two children in a small boat.

The sea was very rough and they seemed to be in trouble. So he flew over to see what was happening.

A little girl was scooping water from the bottom of the boat while her brother tried to row.

'Quickly!' he cried. 'You'll have to go faster than that. We're sinking!'

Septimus hurried back to the harbour to see if he could get some help.

Two men were talking to each other outside the lifeboat station.

Septimus flew round and round, flapping his wings and trying very hard to attract the men's attention.

Just at that moment another man came running out of the lifeboat station and fired two maroons.

Septimus watched the men getting ready to launch the lifeboat. He heard them say that two young children were missing.

Septimus wondered why the children were out at sea in such a small boat on their own.

Then he heard a lifeboatman say that the children had been playing near the beach, but a strong wind had blown up and swept their boat out of the harbour.

Meanwhile, from all over the town, other members of the lifeboat crew heard the maroons exploding. They came running down the streets to help with the rescue.

Septimus hopped up and down on the wall. He was very excited as he watched the lifeboat going into action.

As the lifeboat raced out of the harbour, Septimus flew in front.

'I'm sure that gull knows where the children are,' said one of the crew. 'Quick! Follow that bird.'

As soon as the children had been spotted, Septimus flew down on to the lifeboat.

'There you are' said the lifeboatman, 'I knew that gull would show us the way.'

Just as the lifeboat got near, a big wave crashed on to the children's boat and turned it upside down.

'Hurry! Please hurry!' came the desperate cries. 'We can't hold on any longer.'

Soon the strong hands of the lifeboat crew had pulled the children to safety.

Septimus was delighted. He watched the children being rescued, then followed the lifeboat as it headed back to the harbour.

Back at the lifeboat station, a big crowd was waiting to see the lifeboat come home.

The children's parents ran to meet them. 'We've been so worried,' they said. 'You should have told us where you were going.'

Then one of the lifeboat crew held up a lifejacket. 'And remember, children – if any of you are going out in boats, always wear one of these.'

A fisherman came over from his boat and put down a big bucketful of mackerel.

'This is for Septimus,' he said. 'Don't forget that he is one of our heroes too.'

Septimus felt very proud. He picked out a nice fat fish and ate it quickly. Then he remembered Selena's breakfast, and took another one home with him.

Back on the cliffs Selena was running up and down looking very worried.

'Wherever have you been?' she said.

Septimus dropped the mackerel at her feet. 'Rescuing some children,' he puffed.

'Eat up your breakfast, and I'll tell you all about it …'

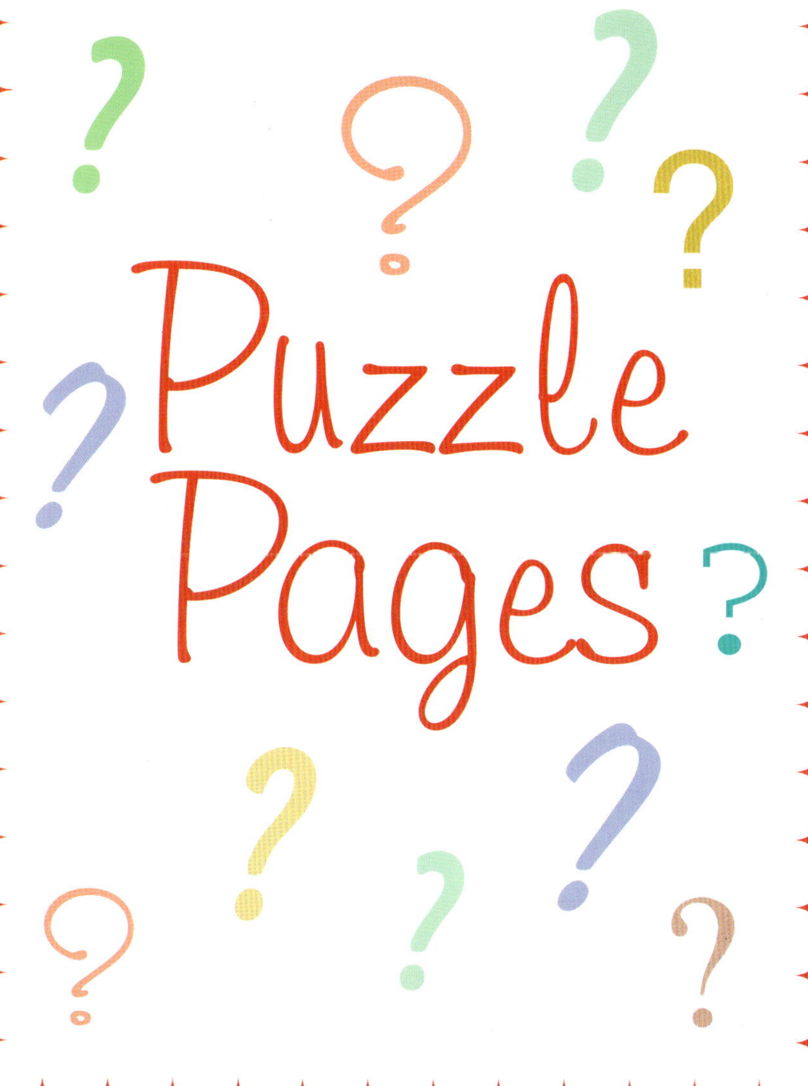
Puzzle
Pages

Tick the correct answers to these questions:

1. When Septimus heard the children crying 'Help', were they:
   a. Playing on the beach?
   b. With their parents?
   c. Out at sea in a boat on their own?

2. Were the special signals fired to call the crew to come to the lifeboat station called:
   a. Fireworks?
   b. Maroons?
   c. Rockets?

3. When the lifeboat raced out of the harbour to rescue the children, was Septimus:
   a. At the lifeboat station?
   b. Flying in front of the lifeboat?
   c. On the cliffs?

4. After the children had been rescued, did their parents say:

   a. You should have told us where you were going?
   b. Were you very frightened?
   c. Are you feeling cold?

5 Did the lifeboatman say the children should have been wearing:

   a. Wellingtons?
   b. Anoraks?
   c. Lifejackets?

6. When Septimus went back to his home on the cliffs he took something for Selena's breakfast. Was it:

   a. A crab?
   b. A mackerel?
   c. A piece of bread?

Join to Septimus all words beginning with "S"

WORDSEARCH

G	U	S	U	M	I	T	P	E	S	U	N
U	V	U	Z	E	N	O	O	A	H	N	U
L	P	R	A	A	E	S	U	C	A	D	M
L	I	F	E	B	O	A	T	H	R	E	L
E	A	R	T	H	H	C	A	E	B	R	S
R	O	A	D	W	A	V	E	S	O	S	M
E	R	I	E	H	H	T	W	O	U	A	A
K	O	R	E	A	S	O	A	L	R	L	T
C	C	I	V	R	I	E	R	O	Y	V	I
A	C	L	I	F	F	S	O	R	B	A	C
M	I	L	L	E	N	N	I	U	M	G	S
L	O	S	E	Z	S	K	I	N	K	E	Y

Can you find all 12 of these words?
SEA, BOAT, CREW, FISH, BEACH, WAVES, CLIFFS, HARBOUR, MAROONS, LIFEBOAT, MACKEREL, SEPTIMUS.
Some letters may be used for more than one word. They can be LEFT to RIGHT, RIGHT to LEFT, TOP to BOTTOM, BOTTOM to TOP or DIAGONAL in any direction.

Join the dots together, starting at number 1 and see what Septimus is doing.

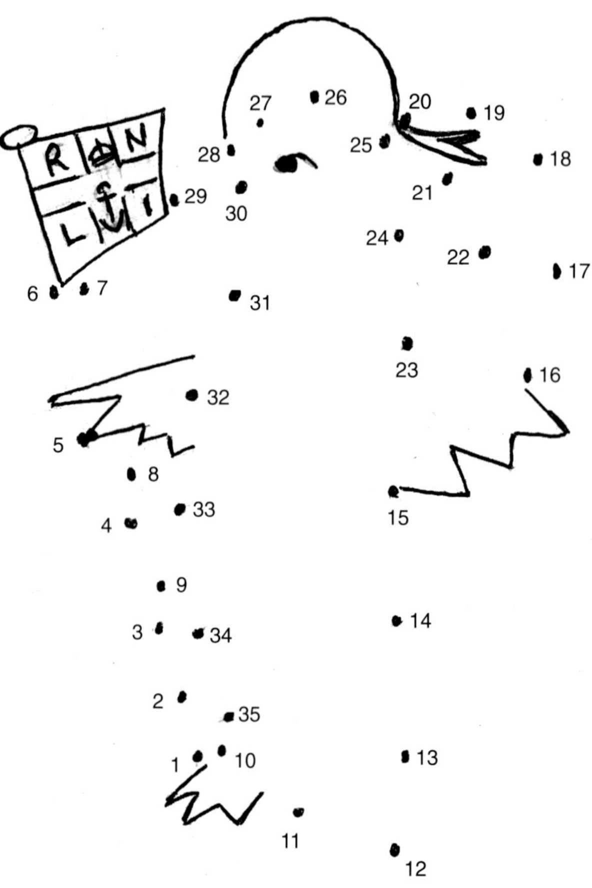

Answers to questions on pages 26 & 27:

Question 1 = c; 2 = b; 3 = b; 4 = a; 5 = c; 6 = b.

Answers to Picture Puzzle, page 28:

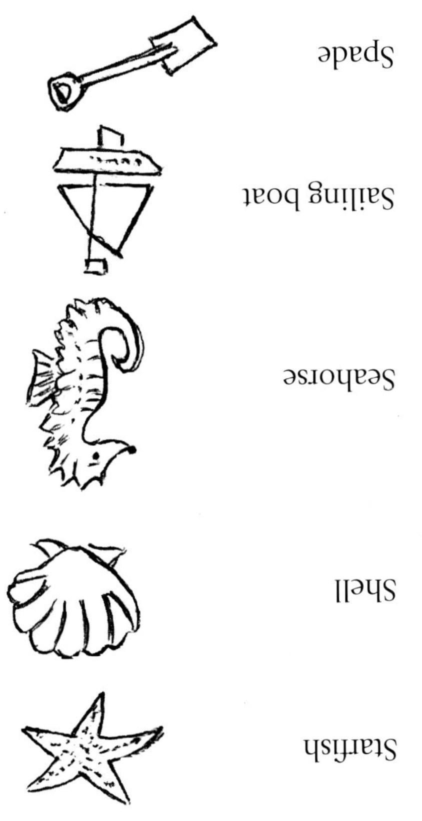

If you would like to join Storm Force, the RNLI's Junior Membership Scheme, please write for details to:

Storm Force HQ,
RNLI,
West Quay Road,
Poole,
Dorset BH15 1XF

Other books in the Septimus Seagull series:

SEPTIMUS COMES TO TOWN
SEPTIMUS MEETS THE SMUGGLERS

Token 1
SEPTIMUS
TO THE
RESCUE